The AQUARIUM Book

Written and Photographed by George Ancona

Clarion Books / New York

To the memory of <u>Ann Troy</u>, my first editor,
whose gentle wisdom guided and encouraged me.

Clarion Books
a Houghton Mifflin Company imprint
215 Park Avenue South, New York, NY 10003
Text and photographs copyright © 1991 by George Ancona
Printed in the USA

Library of Congress Cataloging-in Publication Data
Ancona, George.
    The aquarium book / written and photographed by George Ancona.
      p. cm.
  Summary: Text and photographs depict four major aquariums,
describing how they are able to recreate various aquatic
environments for many species of life.
  PA ISBN 0-395-69940-1   **ISBN 0-89919-655-1**
    1. Marine aquariums, Public—Juvenile literature.   2. Marine
aquariums, Public—Design and construction—Juvenile literature.
3. Aquariums, Public—Juvenile literature.   4. Aquariums, Public—
Design and construction—Juvenile literature.   [1. Aquariums,
Public.]   I. Title.
  QL78.5.A53   1991   90-33328
  639.3′4—dc20   CIP   AC

HOR 10 9 8 7 6 5 4 3 2

Below the surface of the seas is a marvelous living world, a world most of us never see.

The few who do—divers and scientists—share their discoveries with us. To explore this watery universe, we can visit an aquarium.

The marine experience often begins outside the aquarium building. The National Aquarium in Baltimore resembles an abstract ship overlooking the harbor. A fountain with a sculpture of leaping dolphins welcomes visitors to the New England Aquarium in Boston.

4

An awning shaped like a sail stretched
in the wind protects the entry to the
New York Aquarium in Coney Island.

Indoors, the aquatic world opens up
to the visitor. Inside the entrance to the
Monterey Bay Aquarium in California,
replicas of giant whales soaring overhead
leave no doubt that an underwater
adventure is about to begin.

The sight and sound of huge bubbles rising in glass columns set the underwater mood in the lobby of the National Aquarium.

In the central space, daylight fades, giving the feeling of a descent into the ocean depths. The lighted exhibits glow in the darkness. The recorded sounds of ocean waves, seagulls, and distant foghorns can be heard as beluga whales swim in the open pool.

At the Monterey Bay Aquarium, natural sunlight filters down through the swaying kelp forest exhibit, heightening the illusion that the visitor is standing on the bottom of the bay.

Jackass penguins
(*Spheniscus demersus*); rockhopper
penguin (*Eudyptes crestatus*)

The braying of the jackass penguins
greets arrivals at the New England
Aquarium. Towering over the penguins
is the cylindrical four-story Giant Ocean
Tank, which holds 180,000 gallons of
seawater. Sharks, sea turtles, and a
multitude of tropical fish are among
the five hundred specimens that
live together in this re-creation of a
Caribbean coral reef.

Sandbar shark (*Carcharhinus plumbeus*);
horse-eye jack (*Caranx latus*)

Barracuda
(*Sphryna barracuda*)

Spadefish
(*Chaetodipterus faber*)

Cow-nose ray
(*Rhinoptera bonasus*)

Hawksbill turtle (*Eretmochelys imbricata*)

Aqua is the Latin word for water, and water is the common link among all the life forms in an aquarium. These are not only fish and marine mammals, but also reptiles, birds, and plants.

Giant octopus (*Octopus dofleini*)

Moon jelly (*Aurelia aurita*)

Red Hook silver dollar (*Myleus rubripinnis*)

Hippo tang (*Paracanthus hepatus*)

Dice shrimp (*Lysmata debeleus*);
banded coral shrimp (*Stenopus hispidus*)

Copper rockfish (*Sebastes caurinus*);
Bearing hermit crab
(*Pagurus beringanus*)

Sea horse (*Hippocambus erectus*)

Rough Lima scallop (*Lima scabra*)

Lipstick tang (*Naso literatus*)

Sand tiger shark (*Odontaspis taurus*)

Lionfish (*Pterois volitans*)

Cowrie (*Cypraea sp.*)

Unicorn tang (*Naso unicornis*)

Striped surf perch (*Embiotoca lateralis*);
green sea anemone (*Anthopleura xanthogrammica*)

French angelfish (*Pomacanthus paru*)

Yellow-headed jawfish
(*Opistognathus aurifrons*)

Leather star
(*Dermasterias imbricata*);
giant sea star
(*Pisaster giganteus*)

11

An aquarium visitor can travel from the warm tropical seas of the equator to the frigid waters of the Arctic and Antarctic without leaving the building. Exhibits are designed to duplicate the native habitats of the wildlife displayed in the aquarium so that the animals can live as naturally as possible. If the creatures are comfortable in captivity, they will reproduce. This enables aquariums to save some endangered species from extinction.

The puffins at the National Aquarium live in the Icelandic Sea Cliffs exhibit, a habitat that simulates the temperatures and light and darkness cycles of their home in the wild.

Red Sea sailfin tang (*Zebrasoma veliferum*);
lyre-tailed coral fish (*PseudaAthias squamipinnis*)

Asfur angelfish (*Arusetta asfur*)

Some of the world's most colorful and
exotic fish live in the warm tropical
waters that ring the globe near the
equator. Aquarium designers form rocks,
coral, and driftwood out of fiberglass to
create tropical habitats.

Four-eyed butterfly fish (*Chaetodon capstratus*);
pipe organ coral (*Tubipora musica*)

Purple tang (*Zebrasoma xanthurus*)

Today's aquariums do more than display the fascinating inhabitants of the marine world. They also show the dependence of the many living creatures on water and on one another.

An exhibit in the National Aquarium traces the journey of the rain that falls into an Allegheny pond. Rainwater is carried by the river to the tidal marsh where fresh and salt water meet. Continuing on to the coastal beach, it is then swept out to the waters of the continental shelf.

Many species of saltwater fish use the marshes as a breeding ground, leaving their eggs to hatch in protected, nutrient-rich shallows. In the marsh are fingerlings, or young fish, that will someday live as adults in the deep waters of the Atlantic.

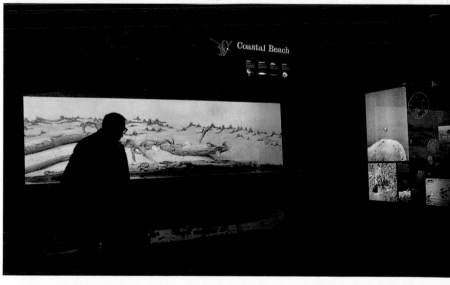

Eating

Different Mouths for Different Diets

Look at the fishes' mouths. Butterflyfish with tweezerlike mouths pick small animals from cracks in coral reefs. Parrotfish have beaks for scraping algae. You may see mouths shaped for nipping and gulping. Hunting at night, the eel uses its sharp teeth to feed on shrimp and octopus.

Eating

Press button below

Aquariums use many media to inform visitors about the exhibits. Drawings, photographs, films, and videotapes make hard-to-see details visible.

Exhibit designers often place different animals side by side to illustrate one theme—for example, defenses against predators. An exhibit shows how the cuttlefish and the balloon fish protect themselves. The cuttlefish burrows into the sand, where the protective coloring on its upper side makes it almost invisible. When threatened, the balloon fish inflates itself with water. Its enlarged size and sharp spines discourage any hungry predator.

Cuttlefish (*Sepia officinalis*)

Balloon fish
(*Diodon holacanthus*)

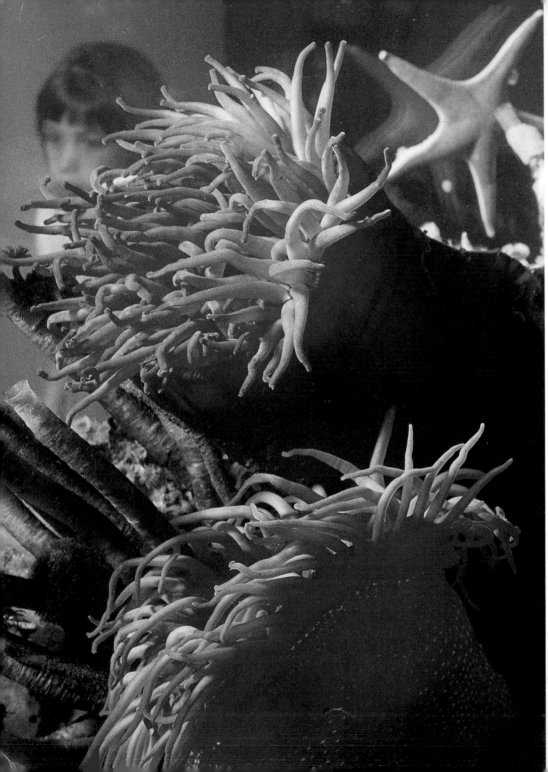

Ocellated clownfish (*Amphiprion occelaris*);
giant sea anemone (*Heterodactylus* sp.)

Strawberry anemone (*Tealis loftensis*);
vermillion star (*Mediaster aequalis*)

Another exhibit shows how different non-swimming species come by their food. Some, like the anemone, wait for food to pass by. Stinging barbs in the tentacles stun the prey, and then the many arms pass the victim to the anemone's mouth. A sea star or starfish uses its hundreds of tiny feet to move about and to bring food to its central mouth.

A living example of a symbiotic, or interdependent, relationship is that of the clownfish and sea anemone. A protective coating allows the fish to live among the anemone's poisonous tentacles. The anemone protects the fish from predators, while the fish protects, cleans, and provides scraps of food for the anemone.

Wharf community

One man's junk is anemone shelter

Like any good neighborhood, the wharf area has a housing shortage. But natural cracks and crannies aren't the only options for living space. Castoff junk provides hiding places for fishes and octopuses; barnacles and others attach themselves to the surfaces. Though these marine creatures are attracted to garbage, littering is still an ugly habit... so don't rush to the wharf to splash your trash.

Onespot fringehead
Neoclinus uninotatus

An old shoe, rusty can or bottle is a fringehead's dream home. Tucked snugly into the junk with just his head poking out, a male guards his castle, ready to charge at trespassers.

diet: invertebrates
size: to 9 in. (23 cm)

White-plumed anemone
Metridium senile

The feathery halo on this animal isn't just for show. Some of the delicate tentacles sweep the water for food; others viciously sting neighboring anemones if they venture too near.

diet: microscopic plankton, particles
size: to 24 in. (61 cm)

Juvenile vermilion rockfish
Sebastes miniatus

You won't recognize these fish in six months when they're grown. Like the violet young rockfish that grow up blue, these red-and-gray juveniles turn vermilion as they mature.

diet: invertebrates, small fishes
size: getting bigger

Sarcastic fringehead
Neoclinus blanchardi

Find the mottled brown fish with a big mouth and you've found the sarcastic fringehead. Protective of its bottle, boot or rubble home on the bottom, this fish isn't above nipping out to nip at a passing diver.

diet: small fishes, invertebrates
size: to 10 in. (25 cm)

Strawberry anemone
Corynactis californica

This animal multiplies by dividing in two. These two divide, too, and the clones keep splitting till they cover a square yard or more.

diet: copepods, larvae, zooplankton
size: to 1 in. (2.5 cm)

Built on the site of a former fish cannery, the Monterey Bay Aquarium focuses on the rich marine life of the bay. One of the exhibits shows how the bay's marine creatures are adapting to the trash that people have thrown into the water.

Outside is the man-made Great Tide Pool, which is open to the bay. It attracts much the same wildlife as any natural tide pool, including harbor seals and sea otters, which drop in for visits. The aquarium staff rescues lost or orphaned sea otter pups and prepares them for survival in the wild. Then they are released into the sea and can return to their homes.

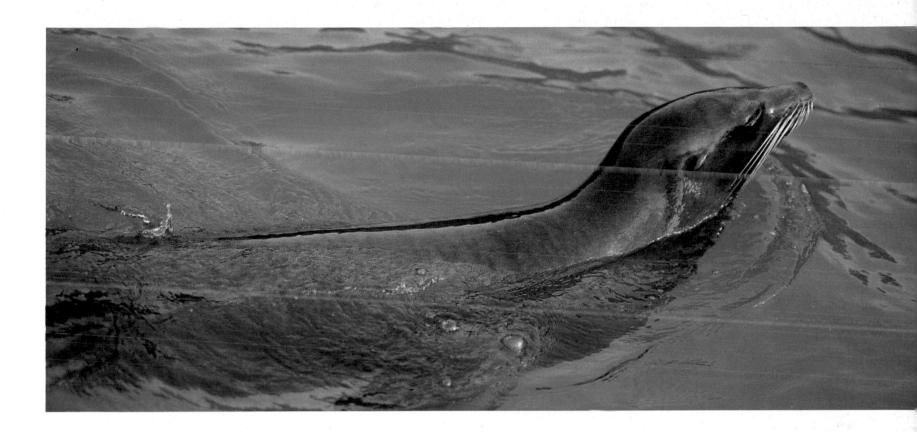

Other outdoor aquarium habitats include the rookery where the black-footed penguins of the New York Aquarium live all year round. In the winter the cold winds from the Atlantic chill the waters of the outdoor pools where the Pacific walrus, beluga whales, and California sea lions are kept. Their thick layers of insulating fat keep them warm while their constant swimming keeps the water from freezing.

The marine environment goes beyond the oceans and seas to include the land around and the air above them. Aquarium displays include animals that don't live entirely underwater but still depend on an abundance of water for their survival.

In the South American Rain Forest growing under the glass roof of the National Aquarium live nearly one hundred tropical birds. The population includes reptiles—frogs, lizards, turtles—and even tropical mammals such as sloths.

Scarlet ibises perch high in the branches of the bamboo trees, where they build their nests. Two ibis eggs have been hatched in the aquarium. Now that many countries prohibit the export of birds, breeding programs like this one have become an especially important resource.

Green parrot
(*Amazona ochrocephala*)

The Sandy Shore Aviary in Monterey is an open-air segment of beach and shoreline. Here shore birds nest, fly, and tiptoe through the gentle machine-made waves.

Gray phalarope (*Phalaropus fulicaria*)

Black-necked stilt (*Himantopus mexicanus*)

Waves are artificially created in indoor exhibits as well. In the Monterey Bay Aquarium's Kelp Forest exhibit, machines create the surge of waves that enables seaweed to absorb the nutrients in the water. In the New York Aquarium four hundred gallons of water are dumped against a rocky shore every forty-five seconds. The water drains into a tide pool filled with urchins, sea stars, and periwinkles. Another exhibit shows how waves are formed and break on a sandy beach.

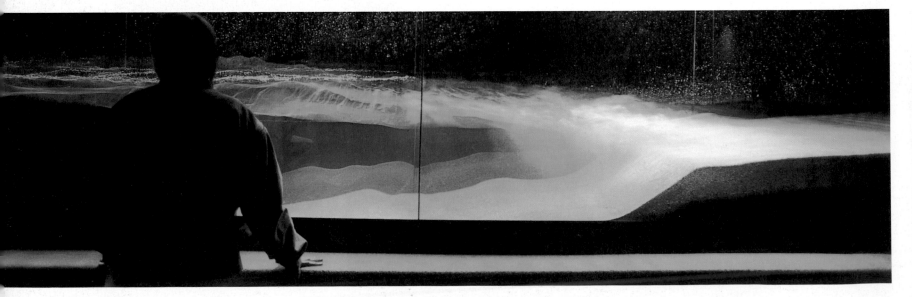

The water in the National Aquarium's closed system is constantly recycled. Salt is added to purified fresh water. The water is filtered three times, and bacteria are added to break down wastes and destroy toxins. Then it is disinfected as it flows under ultraviolet light and through an ozone chamber. Technicians constantly check on the water quality and examine samples for parasites that might harm aquarium animals.

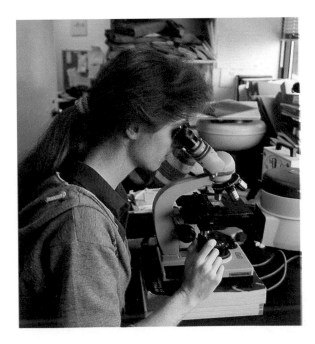

Aquariums are centers of scientific research. The New England Aquarium, for example, is located in a region where lobster fishing is a major industry. Scientists there are investigating the development of lobster eggs. They have re-created natural conditions in the laboratory in order to observe the eggs as they hatch and the baby lobsters as they grow.

People who care for the marine life
in aquariums are called aquarists. By
constantly observing the animals in their
care, aquarists come to know them as
individuals. When a particular shark
needs medication, an aquarist feeds it a
fish with medicine concealed in its gills.
The aquarist must know each shark to
be sure that the medication goes to the
right fish.

Animals must be trained to survive in captivity. Since they cannot fend for themselves, they must learn to depend on people. A trainer handles the octopus once a day. When it has become accustomed to her, it will accept food from her and allow her to draw blood samples to monitor its health.

The birds in the tropical rain forest exhibit are cared for by aviarists. Each species has its food specially prepared. The claws of the yellow-headed blackbird are trimmed every other week.

At feeding times, divers enter the large tanks to feed the fish and turtles. Hand feeding ensures that the smaller, less aggressive fish will get their full share. It also ensures that the predators and larger fish are well fed. Otherwise they would eat the smaller fish in the tank.

Some divers are equipped to talk with the visitors watching them feed the fish. Two-way radios in the divers' masks enable them to respond to questions from the people outside the tank.

Feeding the marine mammals by hand is an opportunity for close contact between the animals and their trainers. It keeps the seals and whales alert and is entertaining to the public. On the lower level of the Baltimore aquarium the beluga whales romp with their trainer while he feeds them. Outside in the seal pool he tosses fish to the sea lions, seals, and walruses.

In the Aquatheater of the New York Aquarium, trainers work with the marine mammals that have learned to perform. Dolphins, sea lions, beluga whales, and the Pacific walrus respond to signals, whistles, and commands.

Sea lions use their whiskers to sense the world around them. Trainers work with this natural behavior when they train a sea lion to balance a ball on its nose, rewarding it with a fish every time it succeeds.

Not all aquarium specimens are kept at a distance or behind glass. Small tide pool exhibits in the Monterey Bay Aquarium are open so that visitors can stick their hands into the water and pick up sea stars, urchins, and decorator crabs. Docents, volunteers who guide people through the exhibits, see that the specimens are handled carefully.

Docile bat rays in a shallow pool have had their stingers removed so that they may be stroked as they glide by.

In other exhibits, magnifying glasses and microscopes are provided to give a closer look at tiny marine creatures.

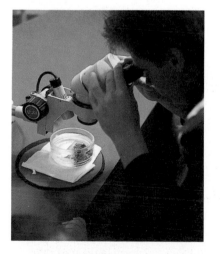

At the aquarium we can share the discoveries of others—divers, researchers, aquarists, trainers, technicians, and many more—and make discoveries of our own. Water covers most of our planet, and the living wonders to be found there invite us to come exploring again and again.

Index

A Select List of Aquariums in the United States

Many zoos also have aquariums. The American Association of Zoological Parks and Aquariums publishes a biennial directory of its members; check the reference section of your library.

Monterey Bay Aquarium
886 Cannery Row
Monterey, CA 93940
(408) 648-4800

Sea World of California
1720 South Shores Rd.
San Diego, CA 92109
(619) 222-6363

Marine World Africa USA
Marine World Pkwy.
Vallejo, CA 94589
(707) 644-4000

Mystic Marinelife Aquarium
55 Coogan Blvd.
Mystic, CT 06355
(203) 536-9631

Sea World of Florida
7007 Sea World Dr.
Orlando, FL 32821
(407) 351-3600

Waikiki Aquarium
2777 Kalakaua Ave.
Honolulu, HI 96815
(808) 923-5335

Sea Life Park
Makapuu Point
Waimanalo, HI 96795
(808) 259-7933

Maine Aquarium
Route 1
Saco, ME 04072
(207) 284-4511

North Carolina Aquarium—
   Fort Fisher
Hwy. 421 South, P.O. Box 130
Kure Beach, NC 28449
(919) 458-8257

Ak-Sar-Ben Aquarium
R.R. 1
Gretna, NE 68028
(402) 332-3901

New York Aquarium
Boardwalk & West 8th St.
Brooklyn, NY 11224
(718) 265-3400

Aquarium of Niagara Falls
Niagara Falls, NY 14301
(716) 285-3575

Sea World of Ohio
1100 Sea World Dr.
Aurora, OH 44202
(216) 562-8101

Gavins Point National Fish Hatchery
   Aquarium
R.R. 1, Box 293
Yankton, SD 57078
(605) 665-3352

John G. Shedd Aquarium
1200 S. Lake Shore Dr.
Chicago, IL 60605
(312) 939-2426

Aquarium of the Americas
1 Canal St.
New Orleans, LA 70130
(504) 861-2537

National Aquarium in Baltimore
Pier 3, 501 E. Pratt St.
Baltimore, MD 21202
(301) 576-3800

New England Aquarium
Central Wharf
Boston, MA 02110
(617) 973-5200

Texas State Aquarium
P.O. Box 331307
2710 North Shoreline
Corpus Christi, TX 78463
(512) 881-1200

Dallas Aquarium
P.O. Box 26193
Dallas, TX 75226
(214) 670-8441

The Seattle Aquarium
Pier 59, Waterfront Park
Seattle, WA 98101
(206) 625-4358

This book would not have been possible without the gracious help of many people, beginning with Ann Troy, who encouraged me to begin the project, and my son Tom, who introduced me to Peter Chermayev of Cambridge Seven, the architectural firm that designed the Baltimore and Boston aquariums. To Vicki Aversa and Jennifer Price of the National Aquarium in Baltimore; Vickie Corliss and Dick Lyons of the New England Aquarium; Lew Garibaldi, Rick Miller, Paul L. Sieswerda, and Frank Greco of the New York Aquarium; Ken Peterson of the Monterey Bay Aquarium; and to all the personnel of the four aquariums who so graciously shared their knowledge with me…

Thank you.